RAILWAY STATIONS

MASTERPIECES
OF ARCHITECTURE

CHARLES SHEPPARD

SMITHMARK

This edition published in 1996 by SMITHMARK Publishers,
a division of U.S. Media Holdings, Inc., 16 East 32nd Street, New York, NY 10016.

SMITHMARK books are available for bulk purchase for sales promotion and premium use.
For details write or call the manager of special sales,
SMITHMARK Publishers, 16 East 32nd Street, New York, NY 10016; (212) 532-6600.

This book was designed and produced by Todtri Productions Limited
P.O. Box 572, New York, NY 10116-0572 FAX: (212) 279-1241

Printed and bound in Singapore

Library of Congress Catalog Card Number 96-68167
ISBN 0-7651-9941-6

Author: Charles Sheppard

Publisher: Robert M. Tod
Book Designer: Mark Weinberg
Production Coordinator: Heather Weigel
Senior Editor: Edward Douglas
Project Editor: Cynthia Sternau
Assistant Editor: Linda Greer
Editorial Consultant: Hilary Scanell
Picture Researcher: Natalie Goldstein
Desktop Associate: Michael Walther
Typesetting: Command-O, NYC

PICTURE CREDITS

AKG Photo, London 6, 7, 35 (bottom)

Arcaid
Alex Bartel 5, 66-67, 78-79
Richard Bryant 64, 70
Mark Fiennes 18
Martin Jones 13
Nick Meers 19 (bottom)
Paul Raferty 69 (top), 72-73

Architectural Association
Alan Chandler 45 (bottom)
Richard Glover 38
Michael Kim 44
Zbigniew Kosok 42 (bottom)
Alistair Viner 46 (top)

Art Resource, New York
Bridgeman 8-9
Giraudon 4, 11 (top), 27 (bottom)
Erich Lessing 24

Bavaria Bildagentur
Fullenbach 34
Mollenhauer 32, 35 (top), 68
Otto 36 (top)

Bibliothèque Nationale, Paris 10, 27 (top)

Bullaty Lomeo 29 (top)

Centre Pompidou, Paris 22, 26, 31 (bottom), 46 (bottom)

The Cincinnati Historical Society 62, 63 (top, bottom left & bottom right)

Fotostock BV, Amsterdam 40-41
Foto Geniek 39
Robert Paul Van Beets 77 (bottom)
Dirk Visbach 76
Tom Weerheijm 74, 75

FPG International 37, 45 (top)
Lee Balterman 43
Farrell Grehan 23
Yoichiro Miyazaki 36 (bottom)
Vladimir Pcholkin 30 (bottom)
Ken Ross 30(top)

Patti McConville 55 (bottom), 56-57, 58

Milepost 92 1/2 11 (bottom), 12 (top & bottom), 15, 16,
19 (top), 20 (top & bottom), 21, 69 (bottom), 77 (top)

Museum of the City of New York 50 (top & bottom), 54, 55 (top), 59

Nawrocki Stock Photo 33

New England Stock Photo
Dodge Photography 52
Frank Siteman 51

Photo Network
Chad Ehlers 28, 71
T. J. Florian 49
Stephen Saks 65

The Picture Cube
David Ball 40 (bottom left) 47
Thomas Craig 42 (top)
P & J McGrath 31 (top)

Picture Perfect 14, 17

Roger-Viollet, Paris 29 (bottom), 40 (top left)

Unicorn Stock Photos 53 (top)
Tom Corner 61
James L. Fly 60 (bottom)
Andre Jenny 60 (top)
Charles E. Schmidt 53 (bottom)

UPI/Bettmann 48

CONTENTS

INTRODUCTION

Until 1830, transportation as we know it today did not exist. Land journeys were made either on horseback or by coach and journeys of a hundred miles would take days. Even by stagecoach, with fresh horses continually replacing the tired animals, such a journey was likely to be an epic adventure—uncertain, arduous, and often affected by mud and weather.

The only way of carrying goods was by horse-drawn cart or water; sailing ships traveled across the seas, and smaller vessels and barges plied the inland waterways. Seaports became the great merchandise centers of the civilized world, and over the centuries European cities grew alongside the ports, which were focal points for transportation, with barges and carts bearing local goods for export or collecting and distributing arriving cargoes.

The cities of the New World were similarly founded on rivers where ocean-going ships could go no further and cargoes had to be transferred. By 1800, most large cities were located at a point of interchange between the sea and the land. Inland towns relied on the horse and cart, and occasionally barges, to supply their needs, so most old towns in Europe were 12 to 20 miles (20 to 32 kilometers) apart—a day's trip to market and back.

The nineteenth century has often been called the Age of Iron, but for centuries before, iron had been smelted and used by village blacksmiths to make horseshoes and line cart wheels. What was new were the industrial-scale techniques enabling iron to be used to make boilers that could withstand high steam pressure. When this technology was combined with the ability to forge accurate pistons, the pressure could be turned into mechanical work; thus the steam engine was born.

The first steam engines were static; by 1800, these were in common use for work like pumping flood water from the Cornish tin mines. The new machinery accomplished tasks that would have taken men or horses hours or days, or simply been physically impossible. Early steam engines weighed many tons, and to become mobile under their own self-generated power they had to have tracks to run on—they would otherwise become stuck or literally bogged down. Such tracks were already in use in mines and factories, where horses pulled heavy loads on iron tracks fixed to the ground by wooden cross ties. But this type of track was expensive, as well as slow to build. It required not only investment of money but also the agreement of all the landowners along the proposed route (parliamentary statutes were needed before the British railway network could be built).

It was only when mass-manufacturing techniques made steam engines and rails efficient and cheap to produce that people began to see the possibilities—and the results—of

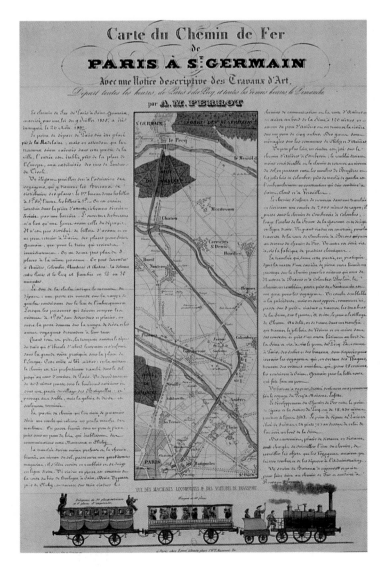

ABOVE: A railway map from 1837 shows the route and transportation available from Paris to Saint-Germain.

RIGHT: Statues grace the facade of Paris' Second Gare du Nord, an elegant Italian "villa" style station under construction from 1861 to 1865.

locomotive power. In 1825, George Stephenson's *Locomotion* hauled thirty-two open wagons carrying over three hundred people and twelve coal wagons the 20 miles (32 kilometers) between Stockton and Darlington, reaching a speed of over 15 mph (24 kph). Stephenson's *Rocket* in 1829 and the opening of the Liverpool and Manchester Railway in 1830 inaugurated the railway age; within fifteen years more than 1,500 miles (2,400 kilometers) of track had been laid.

The railways were to reshape the geography of continents. During the next fifty years, railway networks linked together most of Europe, and the cities of the eastern seaboard of the United States. Inland cities could now trade and manufacture on the same scale as ports; those close to the raw materials of iron, coal, and limestone had particular manufacturing advantages. As railways opened up inland Britain they linked towns such as Birmingham to ports and overseas markets. In America, the railways spread from the East across the Appalachians to link up to the Mississippi Basin and its riverside cities, and then to the ports on the Great Lakes, where

BELOW: An American locomotive of the 1860s steams swiftly towards its destination. By the 1860s railways had spread through both Europe and North America. These rapid advances in technology led to other changes, such as the strategic uses of railways during the American Civil War, the first time such methods had ever been employed.

ABOVE: From the earliest days, railways transformed not just the means of transportation but the city, the country, and the continent. Trains and their engines became emblems of the new era, and the buildings which housed them were called the "cathedrals" of the new age.

Chicago became the staging post for the opening up of the continent. Later the railways linked the Pacific with the Atlantic, truly unifying the continent.

The scale of towns and cities had not changed since ancient times, nor had basic human needs. A large population requires food, and in the era before refrigeration, provisions had to be fresh. A city depended for supplies on its hinterland, particularly the area within a day's carting radius. The agricultural produce of such a limited (and fixed) acreage set a restriction on the size of cities. The railways removed this constraint: By 1850, fish could be sold fresh and in bulk hundreds of miles (200 to 300 kilometers) from the shore. The factories of the Industrial Revolution depended on the railways to bring them materials and to export products. They also needed workers. Cities grew to house the workers needed by the factories, and the new railways carried food and material goods to support the growing populations of the developing urban areas.

Railways transformed not just the means of transportation but the city, the country, and the continent. Trains and their engines became emblems of the new era, and the buildings which housed them were called the "cathedrals" of the new age. This type of building presented an entirely new challenge for architects and engineers, for thousands of passengers had to be directed to the right train on the right platform and stations had to accommodate their movements as well as the great trains, their sheds, and tracks. Nothing like a railway station been ever been built, or needed, before.

CHAPTER ONE
EARLY DEVELOPMENTS

The first station builders had a choice of three materials. Masonry was traditionally used for large buildings such as palaces and churches, but it was slow to build with, and expensive. Its virtue was that it lasted a long time. Timber, on the other hand, was quick and cheap. Although often associated with unpretentious buildings like houses and farm sheds, it was also used on a grand scale as a structural roofing material. And in 1830 the structural use of iron was not new—it had already been used for the Coalbrookdale Bridge, but few builders had experience working with it.

What sort of building was a station to be? It had to be large, to house the mighty steam engines and their iron tracks, and shelter and direct the disorganized bustle of all the arriving and departing passengers, their baggage, and sometimes even their livestock. In the early 1800s no single space compared in scale and height with the archetypal cathedral, although seventeenth- and eighteenth-century palaces, such as Louis XIV's at Versailles, might vie with them for overall size. St. Sophia, in Istanbul, at 250 feet (76 meters) by 107 feet (33 meters) wide and 180 feet (55 meters) high at the crown, was probably the

BELOW: William Powell Frith's painting (1862) is modeled after Paddington Station, London. Here is all the bustle of a big station, complete with fond farewells, errant children hurriedly retrieved, baggage carts, and a dog. Luggage is being stowed on the carriage roofs—a custom left over, perhaps, from stagecoach days.

largest enclosed space in existence at the time. Although serving a humbler purpose, railway stations needed to be built to a similar scale.

The First Stations

The first stations were of wood, built quickly in the 1830s in hasty response to the new demand, using established carpentry techniques. Isambard Kingdom Brunel, one of the earliest of the great engineers and the genius of the Great Western Railway, built the station roofs at Bath, and that at Temple Meads, Bristol, with a span of 72 feet (22 meters). He opted for a hammer beam timber construction which echoed that of the similarly sized roof of the medieval Great Hall of the palace of Westminster. The span is reduced to the minimum needed to cover the tracks by placing the columns on the outer edge of the platforms. Brunel showed that the ecclesiastical formula found in so many medieval churches—of a hall with aisles on either side—could be used to join relatively small spans together to cover several parallel tracks. Despite their medieval ancestry, Brunel's roofs had a modern feel due to the incorporation of extensive roof glazing, now technically possible for the first time.

The early stations were perpetual building sites as new tracks were laid and existing installations adapted and expanded. The confusion was made worse by the different classes of passenger. The rich and aristocratic often insisted on their own railway coaches; sometimes these were even painted in their own livery. An extreme example was the reclusive fifth

Duke of Portland. On his unwilling trips to London from his underground home at Welbeck Abbey, the duke's curtained coach reached the road by means of a one-and-a-half-mile (2.4-kilometer) tunnel specially constructed so that he could come and go unobserved. The entire coach and its invisible occupant were then hoisted onto a railway wagon, allowing the duke to remain unseen until he reached London. At the other extreme were the poor; and in-between the servants, professionals, merchants, and lesser gentry—all unwilling to mix with each other.

In through-stations the waiting halls and offices had to run alongside the platform, parallel to the track. The greater the length, the easier it was for each passenger to alight from his coach or cart opposite his first- or third-class railway carriage, as at Chester or Manchester Victoria. Separating arrivals from departures and the northbound from the southbound by providing a second track and platform opposite helped to sort out some of the confusion. Terminus stations tended to follow the same pattern; even in London the early stations were only a few tracks wide, and the main platform would have been the one closest to the halls and offices.

But the early railway companies saw themselves as the standard-bearers of the new epoch; these hastily built wooden sheds did little to enhance their image. Philip Hardwick and the London Midland Railway had a grandiose idea to remedy this. Their Doric-style Euston Arch completed in 1840 (recalling the triumphal arch built by Decimus Burton in Hyde Park in 1828) symbolized the triumph of the railway and the new

RIGHT: In a project drawing for the Chemin de Fer de la Belgique, Paris, the triumphal gateway follows the lead of the Grand Arch at Euston. The gateway is symbolic of entering or leaving the city, and makes a grand gesture without the complications of having to relate the design to an actual station—here a separate and rather conventional series of sheds and two-story buildings.

ABOVE: Claude Monet's painting of the Gare St. Lazare in Paris captures the atmosphere of rail travel at that time. Beyond the portals of the roof canopy Paris beckons to the traveler with a heady mixture of sun, shade, sky, and mansard roofs.

LEFT: Isambard Kingdom Brunel's classic Gothic station at Temple Meads, Bristol (1839–1841) still stands as a monument to his innovative and harmonious sense of design.

RIGHT: Ironwork construction and detailing are exemplary at York Station and the curve of the roof, which follows the tracks, adds to the visual excitement of the architecture.

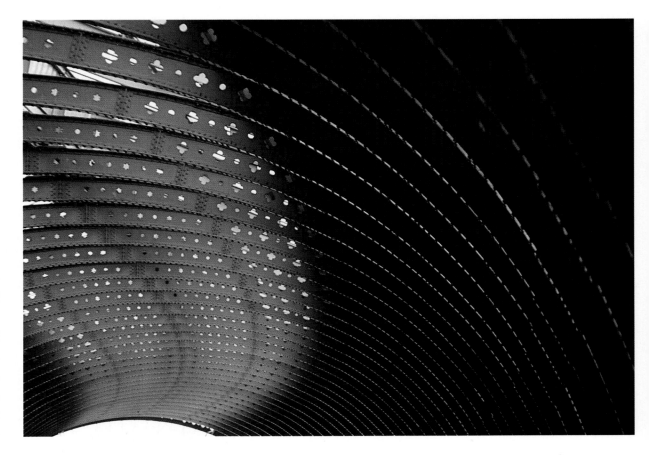

RIGHT: Steel arches span the glazed roof of York's Central Station. The city is famous for its series of grand railway stations, the first of which opened its doors in 1841. This is the third station on the site, built from 1871–1877.

age; it acted as a gateway to the north from London, and a similar but Ionic-style arch in Birmingham heralded the way south. These were also triumphal gates of entry to their cities, and the first monuments of the railway era.

The Heyday of Station Design

Timber was not an ideal material for railway sheds. Steam and soot from coal combustion caused decay and the inconvenience of continuous repairs. Fire was also a hazard. The early sheds were not necessarily seen as permanent structures but as an instant answer to an immediate problem.

The first iron roof was by Robert Stephenson at Euston (platform 6) in 1836; it immediately established a new standard. In 1845 at Newcastle, John Dobson invented a way of rolling iron sections into curves, molding curved ribs and trusses for the first time. His roof arched over three spans, each 55 feet (17 meters), demonstrating the new spatial fluidity of the Iron Age. Height was not just for effect and prestige—under a low roof in a confined space the smoke, steam, and soot would have condensed as dirty rain. The answer was to give the smoke and fumes space to rise and dissipate.

These great enclosures had to be lit, too, in an era before gas lamps and electricity. Glass was the second essential material

ABOVE: The three parallel sheds of Paddington, London, hint at medieval cathedrals as inspiration, and remain a fitting memorial to their engineer Isambard Kingdom Brunel, whose vision was to link London with the New World via the Paddington terminal of the Great Western Railway, the Temple Meads Station in Bristol, and an Atlantic crossing in the *Great Eastern*, then double the size of any other ship afloat.

of the great station roofs. Technical improvements allowed much larger panes and more effective use of roof-glazing—a novelty at the time. The Kew Palm House, built in 1844 by Richard Turner and Decimus Burton, and the Great Exhibition Hall in Hyde Park (1851), with its main hall (by Joseph Paxton) of iron framework with glass infill—literally a crystal palace— defined this new style of building.

It is not surprising that the finest of the early iron sheds is by Digby Wyatt at Paddington (1853–1857); both Wyatt and Brunel, the engineer of the Great Western Railway, were fascinated by the Great Exhibition Hall and its new building techniques. The consistency of design and detailing at Paddington is remarkable, with the feature of transeptal cross-wings adding focus and interest, and emphasizing the cathedral form of the space. The builders' confidence and excitement in the

new materials shines through the whole structure, nowhere more remarkably than in the end window with its free iron-work arabesques.

In 1830, within fifteen years of the first journeys, the railways had become such a universal means of transport that the station at Newcastle required three spans of 55 feet (17 meters); ten years later the iron-and-glass style reached the maturity shown in Paddington, with its triple span of 70, 102, and 68 feet (21, 31, and 21 meters) totaling 240 feet (73 meters).

Equally remarkable is the single span arch of 211 feet (64 meters) at New Street, Birmingham, built in 1854. The railway companies and their engineers favored the single span in spite of its greater engineering demands, as it allowed flexibility for the internal layout, as well as creating a vast impressive space of unprecedented scale. New Street heralded the start of a competition to build the widest span; holding the latest record became a status symbol for the next sixty years, rather like the speed records of the railways or the transatlantic liners.

But there was much more to a station than a great roofed shed. Euston provided another innovation to follow its triumphal arch and prototype iron roof: the great hall. Perhaps stung by contemporary criticism of its arches as a useless extravagance of no benefit to cold and uncomfortable passengers, in 1849 the railway's architect, Philip Hardwick, built a hall more than 60 feet (18 meters) wide next to the train sheds. This was the first enclosed concourse, where passengers could move between booking offices and waiting and refreshment rooms in a space separated from the trains and platforms. This idea, although extravagant, was enthusiastically imitated by later station architects.

Architects and Engineers

By the middle of the century stations had two components: the sheds covering the trains and tracks, which were seen as functional, and the buildings, seen as habitable. At various times both became status symbols for the rival railway companies. Architects had not kept abreast of the new iron and glass technologies; so the rail sheds were designed and built by a relatively new class of professionals, the engineers, who had guided and inspired the use of iron throughout the Industrial Revolution (Telford, Stephenson, and Brunel were the outstanding figures of the first half of the century). But the ticket halls, office, and waiting rooms—the permanent buildings—were often designed by architects. Inevitably, in some stations, the two elements failed to relate; in some cases an intense rivalry even developed between the engineer and the architect. The best stations are the result of close and mutually respectful collaboration, like that between Brunel and Wyatt at Paddington. Sometimes, too, the engineers produced building designs of great civic quality, to complement their sheds, like John Dobson's proposal for a 600-foot- long (183-meter) facade at Newcastle.

RIGHT: Architectural quality and function is maintained even in the ancillary spaces at St. Pancras Station, London. Shown here is the booking hall.

LEFT: Once London's gateway to continental Europe, now Victoria Station is the major collecting point for Gatwick Airport 20 miles (32 kilometers) to the south. Victoria is still one of London's busiest commuter stations, and concourses such as this have typically been widened more than once by terminating the track and buffers further down the line.

While the engineers of the mid-nineteenth century were creating new architectural forms like the crystal palace, the architects were reviving variants of the contrasting classical and Gothic styles, whose respective merits they hotly debated. The facades of Wyatt's neo-Tudor Temple and Meads and Mocatta's classical design at Brighton station exemplify the contrast. At Derby, Thompson built a station facade 1,000 feet (305 meters) long, in Italianate style. Such facades are among the finest examples of civic design of the age, but they had very little to do with the workings of the actual station behind: Indeed, some architects actively tried to conceal the sheds and dissociate their "real" architecture from the modern iron engineering within.

The earliest development on the station site frequently dictated the layout of subsequent additions; so the new buildings generally continued the range of those already built alongside the principal platform. Their bulk was normally minor compared to the size of the rail shed, despite the variety of rooms needed for the various classes of passenger. In the great terminus stations this allowed hotels to be built on several stories at the gable end of the shed(s), often with quite an arbitrary relationship to the station. Many railway companies realized the opportunities offered by incorporating hotels into their station buildings, satisfying the demand for accommodation generated by the railways themselves as well as by the newly enlarged cities. Lime Street Station Hotel in Liverpool (by Waterhouse) is a fine example.

ABOVE: At St. Pancras, Giles Gilbert Scott attempted to elevate the station to the dignity of high art, comparable with churches, town halls, and other civic institutions.

RIGHT: Giles Gilbert Scott's St. Pancras was hailed as a magnificent piece of Victorian architecture, but critics felt that it had little to do with stations or railways. The building here houses station offices and a hotel; the trains arrive in the great shed at the back of the building, which is in the great iron roof tradition.

A Period of Innovation

Lime Street Station also illustrates another trend. During the 1860s the engineers remained obsessed with the idea of ever larger rail sheds and roof spans. Built by Baker and Stephenson in 1867–1868, Lime Street, Liverpool was the first all-iron shed and briefly held the size record, though it was quickly trumped by the rebuilt St. Pancras by Barker and Ordish, completed in 1869. In this magnificent hall, 243 feet (74 meters) wide, 690 feet (210 meters) long, and 100 feet (30 meters) high at the apex, there were no columns: the roof arches sprang from platform level. The engineers resisted the outward thrust from the great latticed roofing ribs with iron tie rods running beneath the elevated tracks.

Perhaps jealous of these accomplishments, the architects produced ever grander designs. Sir George Gilbert Scott's St. Pancras Station Hotel eclipsed them all. Ignoring and screening the station behind, the exuberant detail and picturesque silhouettes made this one of the great Victorian Gothic designs and a landmark in its own right, rivaling the Euston Arch "down the road." With its huge, single-span iron and glass shed and surrounding brick buildings with towers and pinnacles on the grandest scale, St. Pancras was the state of the art in 1880.

But some free spirits went their own way. The hotel at King's Cross was a quite separate building. In 1852, Lewis Cubitt, essentially an engineer, produced an exceptional facade for the sheds of the station itself, with the two great brick arches show-ing the end of the two equal sheds behind (one for departures, the other for arrivals). Such a bold and simple expression of the internal volumes was rare at the time on a civic facade. The station makes a fine contrast with its neighbor, St. Pancras.

The innovative period of station-building in England ends with St. Pancras, although many fine stations were built or extended after this: Cannon Station (Hawkshaw and Barry, 1866), York (Prosser and Peachey, 1877)—memorable for its curving perspectives—Manchester Central (Fowler, 1880), Glasgow Queen Station (Carsewell, 1880), and the Brighton shed (1882). Temple Meads neatly encapsulates early station history: Brunel's timber roof of 1838; the offices and buildings by Fripp in 1852; and the amalgamation, in the 1860s, with a second station which had a fine curved shed and Tudor facade block, both added by Wyatt, built almost at a right angle to the original.

Liverpool Street (engineer E. Wilson, 1875), one of the more unusual and attractive of the later nineteenth-century London stations, is particularly interesting because of its multi-level pedestrian circulation system. This is one of the earliest examples of a solution to a serious layout problem—passenger traffic across the tracks. The station also has immaculately detailed paired columns and roofs, and transepts which unite the different sheds into a continuous space, following the Paddington scheme.

Waterloo (J. R. Scott, architect, and J. Hood, engineer, 1900–1922) was the last of the great stations. Unusual for Britain, it was a new building, double the size of the first station built in 1878 after the terminus moved in from Nine Elms. Waterloo linked the Southern Railway with the Cunard Line's port at Southampton and was thus a gateway to the New World (as Brunel had intended Paddington to be, via the port of Bristol). The glazed roofs running transversely over the tracks are lower than in the nineteenth-century stations, but the overall spaciousness reflects developments on the continent.

LEFT: The simple austerity of Cubbitt's facade at King's Cross, London, has been dissipated by the more recent single-story annex across the front, enclosing additional concourse space. Unlike its immediate neighbor St. Pancras, the facade of King's Cross expresses the twin interlinked sheds within.

LEFT: Here is the St. Pancras Station that only the rail traveler sees. This great single-span iron roof set a benchmark for other stations—and railway companies—to emulate. Paradoxically, in view of the stronger steels becoming available, this was the beginning of the end of such roofs, and multi-span sheds soon became the norm.

BELOW: When completed in 1869, London's St. Pancras Station had the largest single-span roof in the world—243 x 690 feet, 100 feet high (74 x 210 x 30 m). For the next twenty years stations with even larger roofs became status symbols for the railroad companies.

LEFT: The glazed roof of Liverpool Street Station (Edmund Wilson, 1874–1875) is supported by a special system of lightweight steel trusses— a further refinement of the structure used for the second Gare du Nord in Paris.

LEFT: The miles of rail lines snaking through the heart of London were built in the nineteenth century and continue today to serve such modern structures as the new Waterloo Station.

RIGHT: Liverpool Street, London, is a fine example of late nineteenth-century railway architecture. The lattice roofwork, which encloses a fascinating interplay of spaces, has the lightest skeletal structure possible at that period.

CHAPTER TWO

THE GREAT EUROPEAN RAILWAYS

The first rail journeys in France were made within a few days of those in England, and the railway network expanded with similar rapidity. The rest of Europe and the United States were not far behind: The railway age was, indeed, universal.

France

The French developed their railways with characteristic logic and commitment. In the middle ages the great cathedrals, such as Bourges and Amiens, had typically been built over a mere twenty to thirty years, to a single unified design (unlike their equally beautiful, but more haphazard English counterparts). These amazing buildings pushed the stone technology of the time to its limits, and their scale was not exceeded for nearly half a millennium.

This scale, and the consistency of design and execution, was emulated by the imperial autocracy of Louis XIV, as evidenced at the court and palace of Versailles, and by Napoleon Bonaparte (whose defeat at Waterloo was a mere fifteen years before the first railway journey). The French station builders used the same materials and technology as the English, but they were bolder and more forthright. (Isambard Brunel, the most forward-looking and confident British engineer of this period, was half French.) From the outset they had no problem accepting iron as a bona fide building material, neither hiding it nor apologizing for it. Remarkably, they displayed complete assurance in designing with iron, though as a new material it had no accepted architectural language and tradition, in either classical or Gothic styles.

A contemporary engineer, L. Reynaud, expressed the widespread view that "iron forms the rails . . . and should have a part in the building they give rise to . . . to glorify in some way the precious material to which industry has given birth." This sentiment was combined with a willingness and enthusiasm to take the new technology to its limits, whatever those might be.

RIGHT: Works of art can now be seen on display in what was once a great railway station. In the original building of the Gare d'Orsay the vestibule, waiting room, and concourse were all combined in a single space, from which one could observe the trains waiting on the platforms below.

LEFT: This 1865 engraving of the great hall of the North Station (Nord Bahnhof) in Vienna could have come straight out of the portfolio of an opera set designer.

Gare de l'Est

The most remarkable station of the period is undoubtedly the Gare de l'Est in Paris. The Great Exhibition building in London, by Paxton, is generally cited as *the* great early iron building; the Gare de l'Est is its contemporary, built between 1847 and 1852 by H. Duquesney. It is a single large-span shed, using iron throughout. The round-arched form of the rail shed is expressed and emphasized as the centerpiece of the facade design. The huge window formed below throws light into the shed in a manner reminiscent of the great rose windows of French cathedrals, but on a larger scale, as befits an iron structure. This is a station proudly asserting its function and materials, neither pretending to be anything else, nor needing to be hidden behind other flanking buildings. Although it has been considerably extended, the original part survives today. The Gare Montparnasse (V. Lenoir, 1850–1852), almost exactly contemporary with King's Cross, has a similar double arch reflecting the train shed within.

ABOVE: The Paris Métro was among the earliest of the railway developments to serve commuters within a single metropolitan area. Then, as now, new ideas and development frequently provoked opposition and derision. Shown here is A. Robida's caricature of 1889 entitled "The Beautification of Paris by the Métropolitain" (*L'Embellissement de Paris par le Métropolitain*).

PREVIOUS PAGE:
Henri Ottmann's painting of the Gare du Luxembourg in Brussels (1903) shows the vast amount of space occupied by a large railway station—the four-to-five story buildings adjacent seem dwarfed by the vastness of the station approach.

The social upheavals of the revolutionary and Napoleonic eras had freed French society to a small degree from the rigid rules of class. While the plans of the early stations use the same layouts as those in England and give similar consideration to walking distances, both the Gare de l'Est and the Gare Montparnasse integrate the ancillary ticket offices and waiting spaces into the overall design. As in the French cathedrals, there is one overall inclusive design, not the juxtaposition of separate and disconnected elements seen in England.

Gare du Nord

In Britain the terminus plan, with station buildings along one side parallel to the tracks, was seen to give the greatest freedom for future expansion, and large roof spans without columns gave latitude for future alterations to tracks and platforms. But in France, piecemeal rearrangement and expansion were not acceptable. If stations needed to be changed they were rebuilt, on a grander scale and to a similarly defined, formal plan. The first Gare du Nord (engineer L. Reynaud, 1845–1847) was built as a single, unified structure. Within thirteen years, however, it was inadequate to cope with the growth of rail use, and was rebuilt to include extra tracks, again under one great roof space (Hiltorf, architect, and Reynaud the engineer, 1861–1865).

Gare du Nord II is almost exactly contemporary with St. Pancras. The roof is of straight structural members (unlike St. Pancras' latticed arch); this produces a straightforward planar shed roof and a huge gable end, with vertical effect emphasized externally by statues. In contrast, the end of the St. Pancras shed is screened by Scott's hotel (a not altogether

BELOW: A contemporary engraving of the second Gare du Nord in Paris—the classic example of a bold attempt to build a station in which the railshed and passenger accommodation were united in a single architectural form.

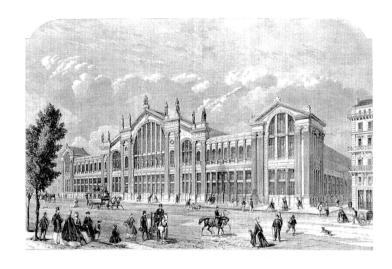

LEFT: Paris in the snow. Prominent in this view of the Gare de L'Est are soldiers on leave. The date is 1917, and the picture by M. Luce (1858–1941) is a reminder that the railways were then harnessed to war purposes, altering military strategy by permitting the rapid mass movement of troops in Europe.

happy marriage when viewed from inside). The French attitude to St. Pancras was predictable and dismissive, punning on their commentary on the Charge of the Light Brigade in the Crimean War: *C'est magnifique, mais ce n'est pas la guerre!* ("It's magnificent, but it isn't war!") became *C'est magnifique, mais ce n'est pas la gare!* ("It's magnificent, but it isn't a station!"). The Gare du Nord is equally *magnifique*—and is proud to be a station. It defined the French terminus form for the next twenty years, and influenced all the later great stations in Paris.

People in Motion

By 1870, Europe had enjoyed an unprecedented period of fifty years' peace and prosperity. The railways had not only met the demand for travel—they had also largely created it. There was now a demand for more trains, larger stations, and more spacious platforms, as well as for a host of service rooms, buffets, and ancillary waiting spaces.

The provision of so many waiting rooms for different classes of passenger was simplified. Arrivals and departures were no longer separated, as shunting empty trains from arrival to departure platforms was a waste of time, space, and manpower. More generous concourse-type space was required, in the manner of Philip Hardwick's Euston Hall. The station was first and foremost a place of *movement*—not just of trains but of people coming and going, moving across

the station to and from arriving and departing trains, ticket offices, and waiting rooms.

This bustling scene was caught by many painters, of whom Claude Monet was the first—although in his work the buildings are a background to the animated foreground of social life. Monet painted several pictures in the Gare St. Lazare in the early 1870s. At the time he was not well known but the station staff were unaware of this. Presenting himself in a rented suit as "M. Monet the painter," he was accorded great respect and civility; he was even asked whether the trains should be shunted round to suit his artistic requirements!

The Gare de Lyon (1897) is one of the finest and most spacious of the later stations. All the details—staircases, doors, and clocks—are fine and solid, in harmony with each other and the whole, neither over-fussy nor crude. Its extravagant clock tower is probably a retort to those built in America. Station clocks became symbols, governing the comings and going of trains and people. Before the railways, nationwide timekeeping was unknown; it was of no consequence if the time varied from one side of the country to another. But the railways demanded a timetable, and a timetable required accurate timekeeping.

The station at the Quai d'Orsay, of similar date to the Gare de Lyon, was the earliest to exploit levels to facilitate passenger movement. The tracks and platforms are below the passenger entrance level, but a single, finely decorated barrel-vault roof

RIGHT: Width, breadth, and simplicity characterize the second Gare du Nord in Paris. The early French designers and engineers accepted iron as the proper material and were not afraid of the logical answers to station building; the large span of roof trusses on minimal columns allowed the greatest freedom of layout for tracks and platforms.

ABOVE: The Gare de Lyon is one of the most spacious of the nine-teenth-century Parisian stations, and from the great engineered roof trusses to details such as the clock it demonstrates an architectural unity.

LEFT: The interior of the Gare d'Orsay at the Quai d'Orsay in Paris, as it appeared in 1902. This gracious station, now a museum, was designed by Victor Laloux and timed for the opening of the Paris Exposition in 1900.

BELOW: The interior of the Musée d'Orsay, Paris. Here the vaulted roof and skylights of the old station have been put to good use in a museum setting.

spans both in one space. Lit by high-level windows, this was a prototype of later concourses.

In the provincial cities stations were not on the grand scale of those in Paris, but in the later years of the century some stations were built with fine facades, reflecting the variety of architectural styles prevailing at the *fin de siècle*. The facade at Tours (1895–1898) is notable, while Limoges, although later, has a splendid domed cupola roof inside. Metz may boast the only station designed by a monarch; it is suggested that its rather ponderous facade may originate from the Prussian Kaiser Wilhelm after he annexed Lorraine in 1871. Antwerp's (1890–1898) decorated facade has octagonal turrets complemented internally by a single huge shed—the finest in Belgium.

The great French contribution—the development of an "iron style"—was carried across the century in the Art-Nouveau entrances designed by Hector Guimard to the underground Métro system in Paris.

RIGHT: Not all great railway stations still serve their original purpose. The Musée d'Orsay in Paris, was once the Gare d'Orsay, a model station that served the trains of the Orleans line.

The Close of the Century

By the last two decades of the nineteenth century, some of the defects of earlier stations had become all too apparent. Designers consistently underestimated the success of the railways; as the platforms and circulation spaces became wider, so the number of passengers and trains increased, but the resulting bustle and confusion remained fairly unchanged.

The great roofs were also a problem. Much larger spans than that at St. Pancras were needed to cover the increased number of tracks and platforms now required to be under one huge "umbrella." As the public came to accept railways—and stations—as a part of everyday life, designers became less obsessed with showing off stations as symbols of the new age. With a standard gauge and rationalized practices, fewer alterations and layout changes in platform and track were now needed, and flexibility of layout under one huge roof no longer offset the cost of repairs. The replacement of a small column supporting a light load in a multi-span shed was comparatively simple, and needed only simple propping; repairs to the structural members of large-span roofs were much more disruptive and difficult. So designers now came to prefer smaller spans such as those built a half-century earlier at Euston and Paddington.

This change of strategy perversely came at a time when technical advances had dramatically increased the area that could be covered with one span. This structural leap forward was made possible by the growing use of steel in place of iron. Even early steel could be alloyed to yield different properties; its strength was much greater than that of iron, and it could be given greater resistance to corrosion and rust. Steel had been in use since the mid-1870s; the Galerie des Machines at the Paris Exhibition of 1889 (which also featured the Eiffel Tower) achieved a span of 377 feet (115 meters). By the time steel had become the vogue, the railway networks of France and Britain. had reached a maturity where few new stations were required.

ABOVE: The facade of Tours Station continues the French tradition of expressing the "age of iron" with fine arched gables. A sense of civil dignity is added by the massive stone abutments crowned with statuary.

BELOW: This 1903 project drawing for a Parisian railway station offers a monumental concourse beneath the pyramid roof. There are minaret towers and cupolas in abundance, a drive-through porte-cochère for taxis, entrances and canopies on three sides, and a splendid succession of projecting plinths.

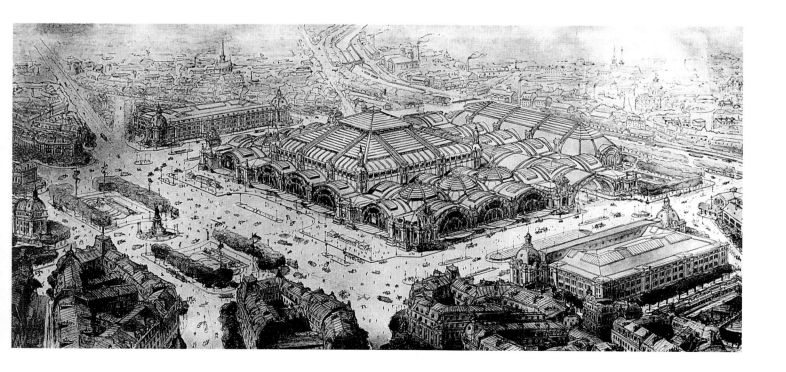

Germany

The unification of Germany under Bismarck, from the middle of the century, gave the impetus to change and the stimulus for growth which led to the great new steel stations of the large industrial German cities.

In Germany, railways and stations had by now spread across the country. Among the pre-steel stations, the facade of Brunswick (Ottmer, 1845) is a typical piece of civic design, rather in the tradition of the Great Hall at Euston, with little external indication that it is a station. (It has recently been used as a bank.) Other fine stations in the pre-steel decades built in the twin capitals of Austria–Hungary date from 1870 (Vienna West Bahnhof, Bäumer), 1873 (Budapest West, Eiffel), and 1881 (Budapest Ost, Rochlitz); and the Centraal at Amsterdam, Holland (1881) has a fine two-bay barrel roof and magnificently decorated facades by Cuypers, the leading Dutch architect of this period.

The Cross-Platform

As trains and stations became bigger and the number of platforms multiplied, passengers had to walk even further to reach their trains. In the early terminus layouts, such as at Paddington or Berlin Stettiner (Stein, 1876) the ticket halls and waiting rooms tended to run alongside one of the side platforms. The distances to the furthest platform on the opposite side became ever larger, and the distance was now harder to negotiate with baggage as arrivals and departures were no longer separated. More space and width were needed on the platforms themselves, and, more importantly, on the linking cross-platform across the head of the tracks.

Zurich in Switzerland currently illustrates this increase in size and functional requirement. The original Waner station of 1865 had buffets and offices along one side. The later development took advantage of the side approach and built a new crossway across the end of the old shed, effectively abandoning the old station and constructing an entirely new one with two or three times the number of platforms further down the track. In the great German stations this cross-platform, or crossway, became the focal point, with the ancillary halls and spaces, entrances, and exits all relating to it.

Frankfurt (Georg P. H. Eggert, 1879) set the scale for these later stations. Three huge sheds (one for each of the old regions formerly served by three separate stations), each with a span of 183 feet (56 meters), were set side by side; the resultant multiple shed, with fully glazed roof, was 610 feet (186

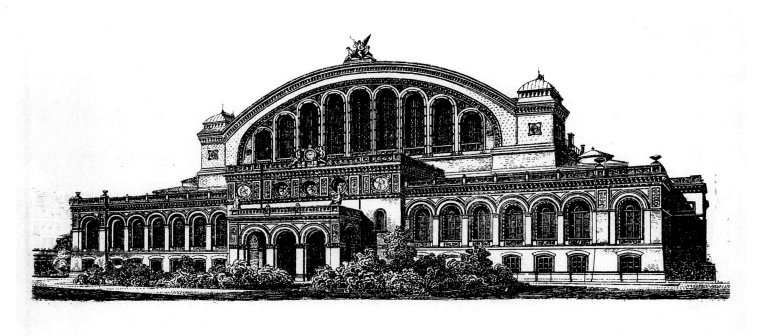

LEFT: As is often the case, historic nineteenth-century railway buildings now share their setting with modern urban edifices. Shown here is the station at Hannover–Niedersachsen.

ABOVE: The facade of the Berlin Hauptbahnhof is a clear statement of its internal organization. A modest front portico indicates the entrance; behind is clearly a long concourse, or cross-platform running across the ends of all the tracks. Dominating from behind is the vast cable and the barrel-vaulted roof enclosing the train shed.

meters) long by 550 feet (168 meters) wide, and topped 93 feet (28 meters). To ease the pedestrian confusion, there were separate platforms for baggage.

The designers experimented with alternative ways of solving the cross-circulation problem, which was eased where the railway tracks and platforms were at a different level from the arriving or departing pedestrians—as if the railway were in a cutting, or raised on a viaduct. As early as 1840, sloping ground had been used at Bristol in England and at Newport, South Wales, to shorten walking distances. The Berlin Alexanderplatz station in Germany (Johann and Jacobsthal, 1880–1885), exploited the viaduct siting of the (through) station. A glazed curved roof covered tracks and platform on the upper level; at ground level were ancillary spaces, offices, and crossways connected by staircases to the platforms (Berlin Friedrichstrasse shows a similar layout). Such an arrangement is a trade-off: The advantage of shorter pedestrian distance is offset by the inconvenience of the steps.

Elsewhere in Germany, at Dresden (1892–1898), C. F. Muller took full advantage of the viaduct site of the station. The Hauptbahnhof has four great sheds of 100 feet (30 meters), 193 feet (59 meters), 100 feet (30 meters,) and 30 feet (9 meters) covering fifteen tracks, some terminus, and some through stations. The lattice construction of the columnar supporting members allows the space to flow from bay to bay, creating an illusion of infinity.

In Hamburg, Germany (Reinhardt and Sussenguth, 1903–1906), on the other hand, the tracks and platforms are below the passenger arrival level. The cross-platform here is a huge bridge across the tracks, a 240-foot-long (73-meter) concourse with waiting rooms, buffets, booking halls, and other facilities on either side covered with a glazed vault roof. Towers mark each end of this crossway, to denote the station and link it with the town. The whole concourse complex is skewered through the magnificent barrel vault covering the tracks like a cathedral transept, but at a higher level, with glass replacing stone to form a huge iron cage in a glass case. Here the pedestrian circulation and access problem is efficiently solved. The dramatic interplay of spaces inside accords with the station's civic importance, defining the state of the art of the time.

Other fine stations of this period include those at Basle and Cologne. The last of the epoch is at Leipzig (Lossow and Kühne, architects, and Louis Eilers, engineer), begun in 1907 and finished in 1915. This vast structure had six parallel sheds, each almost 150 feet (46 meters) wide, with a separately roofed transept platform itself 80 feet (24 meters) wide across the full width of the tracks. The roofs are surrounded by huge flanking walls and are thus not externally visible.

The First World War put an end to the building of great stations in Europe, as it did to so much else—later work was more concerned with repairs and refurbishment.

RIGHT: The railway station at Hamburg is one of a unmistakable series of structures based on the classic design by Johann Eduard Jacobsthal (1839–1902).

ABOVE: Georg P. H. Eggert's station at Frankfurt am Main, begun in 1879, took nine years to complete. The station, which combined the services of three earlier stations into a single complex, was constructed on what was then the city's outskirts, as no other adequate space could be found.

LEFT: The great station and shed at Dresden was opened in 1898. Designed by the firm of Giese and Weidner, it offered all the conveniences of the period—including easy access to electric trolleys and horse-drawn taxis.

RIGHT: The old-fashioned plaza and station of the Hauptbahnhof at Bremen continue to serve today's travelers in this historic city.

ABOVE: Six parallel vaulted roofs span the tracks of Leipzig Station. Built between 1907 and 1915, this station is one of several in Germany which are the culmination of the steel era in station building.

RIGHT: A period photograph of Anhalt Station in Berlin, dated June 13, 1930—the day that this famous station celebrated its fiftieth anniversary.

Spanning Continents

By 1914, all continents were crisscrossed with iron, and track mileage generally reflected the population density. The motivating force of railway expansion varied from place to place. In America, the westward spread of the tracks unified the East and the Pacific coasts, opening up the countryside. A similar continental railway linked Canada's Pacific coast with the St. Lawrence River and the Atlantic Ocean. In Asia, the Trans-Siberian Railway joined the Pacific and European frontiers.

Sometimes the railway was the means of establishing a political union of territories not possible otherwise, or of executing military control. The sealed train which took Lenin from exile in Switzerland to St. Petersburg in 1917 after Russia's surrender to Germany would not have been possible in a former age—and military strategies would have been quite different if the rapid movement of troops and materials by rail had not been possible. St. Petersburg Station was rebuilt in Lenin's memory.

In the early nineteenth century, merchants in California could only trade bulk goods with the eastern states by daring the storms of Cape Horn. Even after the opening of the Panama Canal in 1905, such trade, and the resulting economic gain, was largely the product of the railways. Railways were sometimes built to exploit mineral wealth in the center of a land mass, as in South Africa, an undertaking that would have been impossible in a pre-railway age.

A spirit of optimism of investing in an assured and better future is inherent in some of this development—like the

RIGHT: A modern cement platform—rather than polished marble or Beaux-Arts ornamentation—greets the arriving or departing passenger at Amsterdam's Central Station.

LEFT: Going beyond the palatial in effect, the interior concourse and roof of Atocha Station in Madrid appear to have been designed for an army of giants.

ABOVE: The central station and surrounding plaza at Anvers, Belgium, shown here in a period photograph, offers a view of several different modes of transportation in an earlier era.

ABOVE: Amsterdam Central Station has an elaborately decorated facade designed by P. J. H. Cuypers. There is a hint, perhaps, of St. Pancras in London, although here there is less of a contrasting break between the facades and the railsheds.

RIGHT: This exterior view of Rotterdam's Central Station shows the complex layout of buildings and trackwork necessary for moving vast numbers of passengers (and freight) from one place to another.

ABOVE: As at Tours, Budapest West Station sandwiches the engineering and iron of the main shed between architecturally symmetrical masonry pavilions. These two approaches are unrelated, but combine to make a fine and imposing facade.

RIGHT: A general view of Yaroslavsky Railway Station, Moscow. The scale and form of stations is dictated by the size of the trains and the number of platforms—the elements of a station are basically the same wherever it is built; regional traditions and ornamentation complete the design.

railway crossing the Andes at Condor, Bolivia, between Rio Mulato and Potosi, built in 1908 and rising to an altitude of 15,700 feet (4,785 meters)—the highest in the world. Elsewhere, railways were built for the tourist trade: in 1880, to view the eruptions of Vesuvius from the volcanic rim at 4,000 feet (1,219 meters), and in 1912, the highest station in Europe (11,330 feet (3,453 meters) to see the Alpine peaks and glaciers at Jungfraujoch.

Regional Architecture

The scale and form of stations is dictated by the size of the trains and the number of platforms—the elements of a station are the same wherever it is built. Uniform materials and technology predicate their own logical structural forms. But the detailed architectural expression can—and does—vary in the same way as in any other building type. Traditional indigenous building styles and climate are, naturally, influences. Moscow Kazan (A. V. Schuser, 1911) is based on traditional Russian styles; the facade is broken up to allow a greater range of expressive detailing. The restaurant inside is in lavish Russian

ABOVE: During the nineteenth century, the boom in rail transportation spread stations across the world. Shown here is a platform and train in the main station of Buenos Aries, Argentina.

Baroque. Spanish stations are influenced by Moorish-derived arches and porticoes, while Portugal has cool mural wall tiling.

Frequently such national or regional features were incorporated in colonial countries. Many of the smaller South American stations show Spanish antecedents. The largest is the Retiro terminus in Buenos Aires by Lauriston Condor, built in the 1920s. This station is impressive by any standards; two roof spaces, each 328 feet (100 meters) wide by 82 feet (25 meters) high, over sheds 820 feet (250 meters) long. Unfortunately the broken facade expresses none of this scale or grandeur.

In India, European styles were amalgamated with local features, and East met West in a fascinating series of stations. Madras (1868) has an ordered, restrained facade, while Bombay Churchgate is a vast fairytale castle surrounded by parkland. But pride of place is most evident at Bombay Victoria (F. W. Stevens, 1887). Externally, the Gothic debt to Scott's St. Pancras is obvious; but many of the details of the composition are in exuberant Saracenic style. It is also remarkable as one of the biggest stations in the world; the interior is dominated by a huge central dome with flanking ancillaries. Mogul-style roof cupolas dominate at Lucknow, while the austere, undecorated facades of Lahore, built soon after the Indian Mutiny in 1857, make no attempt to hide its dual use as a fortress.

The later years of the nineteenth century saw the beginnings of a revolution in architectural design. For one hundred years a battle had raged between the protagonists of the neo-classical and the neo-Gothic. Now the new materials of iron and steel, and new techniques for casting glass, were finally being absorbed into a variety of new approaches and styles. Rapid communications, made possible first by railways carrying mail, and then by the invention of the telephone, transferred ideas and designs, and even materials, rapidly across continents.

ABOVE: The classic steel and glass roof of Milan's Stazione Centrale
(Ulisse Stracchini, 1913–1930) was restored to its full splendor in 1952.

LEFT: A period photograph of Milan's Central Station under construction in the 1930s—the last station in Europe to be built on the grand scale, and also one of the biggest.

BELOW: Exterior of the Stazione Centrale II, Milan: What began as a Beaux-Arts masterpiece in the competition of 1913 had by its opening in 1930 become an unwieldy compendium of monumental excess.

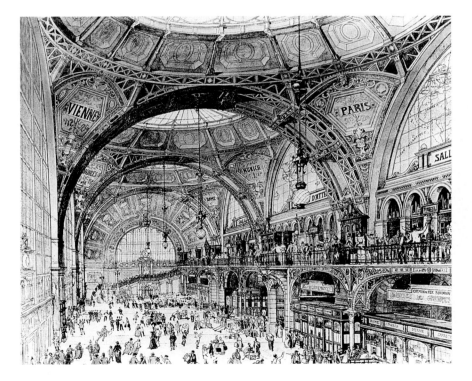

ABOVE: Victoria Terminus, Bombay, pays homage to Scott's Gothic St. Pancras, but with many details in an exuberant Saracenic style. It is one of the biggest stations in the world.

LETF: Alexandre Marcel's 1894 design for the grand hall of the Central Station in Bucharest. The two-level concourse beneath the triple-domed roof is a splendid space, and illustrates the separation of the concourse from the tracks, which was becoming standard by this date.

RIGHT: The Victorian Flinders Street Station in Melbourne, Australia, makes a fine contribution to the modern cityscape.

CHAPTER THREE

THE UNITED STATES AND THE GLOBAL RAILWAY NETWORK

At the beginning of the railway era the settled areas of the United States were mostly on the eastern seaboard, with the population largely concentrated in a 500-mile (800-kilometer) span that included Boston, New York, Philadelphia, and Baltimore. To the west lay the Appalachians, and a considerable distance beyond was the Mississippi Basin, originally settled by river navigation. Still further west the land was increasingly wild. Even in the East the population density was low compared to Europe, and the size of the cities was constrained by the same low level of transportation technology as in Europe.

Vast Distances

The major problem confronting American railway engineers was the vast distance the railways had to cover. The greater the distance, of course, the greater the expense of laying the track,

and the greater number of engineering problems to be overcome—bridges, tunnels, and cuttings.

Simply laying track over these huge distances swallowed up most of the railway-building budget in the early years, and in the New World the niceties and comforts of rail travel had to wait their turn. Perhaps the early railways were appropriate in a pioneering society. Early American stations tended to be small, improvised, rough, and ready, rather like the Euston sheds in the 1830s but on a smaller scale. It took time, and the profits generated by success, for the stations to come to reflect the national importance of the railways themselves.

As they did in Europe, American railways carried imported goods away from the seaport cities and increased the radius of supporting farmland, allowing the cities to grow and industrialize. Their other important function, again as in Europe, was to bring together the raw materials of industry and provide

RIGHT: The American railroad companies vied to outdo each other in the creation of opulent spaces. Stations were seen as status symbols for the rail companies, and architects lost no opportunity to show off their own skills—here, the Romanesque interior of Union Station, St. Louis.

LEFT: New York's first Pennsylvania Station (demolished c. 1964) was focused around a magnificent concourse plaza. The dramatic glass-vaulted roof is in the grand iron and steel engineering tradition.

ABOVE: New York's Grand Central Station I (1871) was the first railway station in the United States to match those in Europe. Externally its architecture was undistinguished. The facade screens the gable end of the great train hall behind.

distribution networks which gave access to trade markets at home and overseas—but again the distances were much greater than in Europe. Coal was plentiful in the Pennsylvania Appalachians, but the great industrial cities that developed at Pittsburgh and Cleveland were remote from the larger markets of the coastal cities.

Despite these problems, or, perhaps, because of them, the railways were crucial to establishing America as a country, first in the East, and later across the full width of the continent. Given this key role, the railways were, from the start, fully integrated with the economic life of the country. The millionaire railroad magnates often owned or had large shares in the distant economic and industrial enterprises their railways served. It has been said that the West was won by barbed wire fencing rather than the revolver, but without the railways how would the wire have gotten there?

Building with Timber

For two hundred years Western Europe had been chronically short of wood. In an era of wooden sailing ships and nations dependent for wealth on trading links (especially with their colonies), this was a serious problem. One covert aim of the famous English landscaping style of the late eighteenth century had been to increase wooded cover, and thus the stocks of timber for ship-building. This shortage of wood encouraged engineers and contractors to try out new materials such as iron. In America, not only were the sources of iron more remote, but stocks of fine timber were also virtually inex-

haustible. It is hardly surprising that Americans went on building wooden stations well after their European contemporaries.

The use of timber did not have to imply pre-mechanized methods. There was an American tradition of off-site manufacture of timber components, such as trussed beams, to standard patterns, often patented, like those of Ithiel Town (1826, 1835). Builders could put up large structures quickly to a standard pattern using small-section timber; this encouraged them to use wooden structures well into the big-span shed era, as at Philadelphia (1851), with its span of 150 feet (46 meters). These wooden structures allowed for the expansion and alteration which characterized the early American stations as much as those in Europe. Iron and steel buildings were only put up when these earlier timber structures proved quite inadequate or fell into serious decay. Patented lattices and trusses in iron and steel, similar to those of timber, were by then available.

A mere twenty years separates the New World's first station at Mount Clare in Baltimore (Baltimore–Ohio Railroad, 1830, with horse-drawn trains) from Great Central Station, Chicago (Howe, 1853), which had an iron roof spanning 166 feet (51 meters). (The station at Mount Clare is still standing, now part of a railway museum with a superbly roofed adjacent roundhouse.) A further thirteen years elapsed before the opening of the first Grand Central Station, New York (Buckhout and

ABOVE: New York's first Grand Central Station initiated an informal twenty-year contest to build the railshed with the largest span; it culminated in the 300-foot (91.5-meter) span of Philadelphia's Broad Street Station. Such was the growth of rail travel that within thirty years of its construction, Grand Central Station was completely rebuilt.

RIGHT: Railways depend on accurate time keeping—on a continental scale. Clocks and clock towers provided the opportunity for sculptural flourish and local or national emblems; shown here is South Street Station, Boston.

Snook, 1869–1871). This was the first of the American stations built with the scale and grandeur to match those of Europe.

Like the nearly contemporary St. Pancras in London, it followed the concept of a single cover-all barrel roof, 200 feet (61 meters) wide by 600 feet (183 meters) long, and 100 feet (30 meters) high. To reduce the nuisance from smoke and steam, harmful to both the building structure and passengers, it was the policy at Grand Central I to shut down the train engines on arrival at the station, and only couple up engines to departing trains at the last minute. Whether or not this policy was effective, this concern to minimize the exposure of passengers to the unpleasant side of rail travel became a typical feature of later American stations—in contrast to its marked absence in the early days. Externally, the station was disappointing; the sheds were screened by buildings whose architecture lacked scale and distinction.

The Big-Span Challenge

Grand Central I was in the tradition of the big-span challenge laid down by St. Pancras, although it was not so wide; subsequently the challenge was taken up by the Pennsylvania Railroad Company, with three great stations each with huge single-span roofs. The first of these was at Jersey City (New Jersey), 1888, with a trussed-arch construction by C. C. Schneider spanning 252 feet (77 meters). At Pittsburgh, the 1898 station had a roof 110 feet (34 meters) high with a 240-foot (73-meter) span; one end of the span was on rollers to allow for thermal expansion. But the greatest single-span shed was at Broad Street in

Philadelphia (Wilson Brothers, 1892–1893), a colossal 300 feet (91 meters) wide, 108 feet (33 meters) tall, and 595 feet (181 meters) long. These three stations were on a scale to match any in Europe. The great rail halls had finally come to symbolize the importance of the railways as the arteries of America, and of the railroad companies themselves.

Other fine wide sheds were built in the 1890s at St. Louis (Link and Pegram, 1891) and Boston. Both these roofs were constructed to look like a single, huge span, although they were really several smaller ones. There were five spans at St. Louis, curiously low, with inverted lower chords, and, more

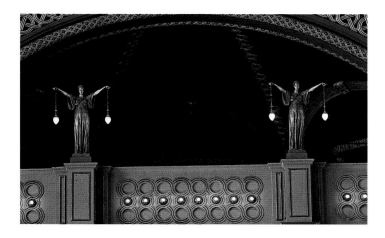

ABOVE: Gilt statues and ordered decoration complement the restrained colors of architect's Theodore C. Link's St. Louis Union Station (1891–1894).

RIGHT: Union Station, St. Louis is a much-loved city landmark that once briefly enjoyed the title of the "largest depot in the world." The colorful roofs of the front buildings screen the unique five-bay roof, seen to the left.

LEFT: The capital and maintenance costs of the great iron and steel roofs eventually became prohibitive. Even large stations now offer waiting passengers little weather protection on the platform itself, as with Boston's South Street Station, shown here.

successfully, three spans at Boston. The three large spans at St. Louis are 130 feet (40 meters); at Boston the main span is more than 200 feet (61 meters). These sheds mark the last attempts at a single-span roof over a whole station complex. Other multiple sheds of the period include Illinois Central, Chicago (B. Gilbert, architect, and J. F. Wallace, engineer, 1892–1893) and New Orleans, 1892, by the most distinguished American architect of the period, Louis Sullivan.

American stations were frequently at the geographic center of cities—often because the city came into existence with the coming of the railroad, and grew up around it. The station was thus a central element in the civic fabric. The twin sheds of the station at Worcester, Massachusetts, are integrated with the 212-foot-high (65-meter) tower into an organized architectural form. External clock towers (such as Detroit, 1882 and Chicago Dearborn, 1883), frequently make a civic contribution as well as defining local time—important in a country large enough to need several time zones.

Urban Planning

European cities have evolved over centuries with streets linked like a series of spiders' webs; in contrast, American cities have been dominated by planned grids of parallel streets. Development pressure naturally intensified on the blocks close to stations, often in prime downtown locations. Stations themselves lost the clarity of their own individual form as they were engulfed in the building boom, and gradually ceased to be identifiably separate buildings. While taking the record for the largest station roof span in its time, Broad Street, Philadelphia was also developed externally to be virtually indistinguishable from the adjacent blocks and buildings. The casual eye outside cannot detect a station at all.

Not all railroad companies involved themselves in this quest for station size and status. When steel became widely available it might have started off a new round of competition; but, just as in Europe, the huge single shed became unfashionable. Perhaps the companies collectively recoiled from both the capital layout and ongoing maintenance of such projects. Inconvenient passenger distances, crowded platforms and crossways, and remote waiting rooms, often a long way from the required train, made large sheds obsolete in America as in Europe.

The architects of the second Grand Central Station in New York (Reed and Stern, 1903–1913) designed it to maximize capacity and minimize user inconvenience. It accommodated sixty-seven tracks with over six hundred trains, and 110,000

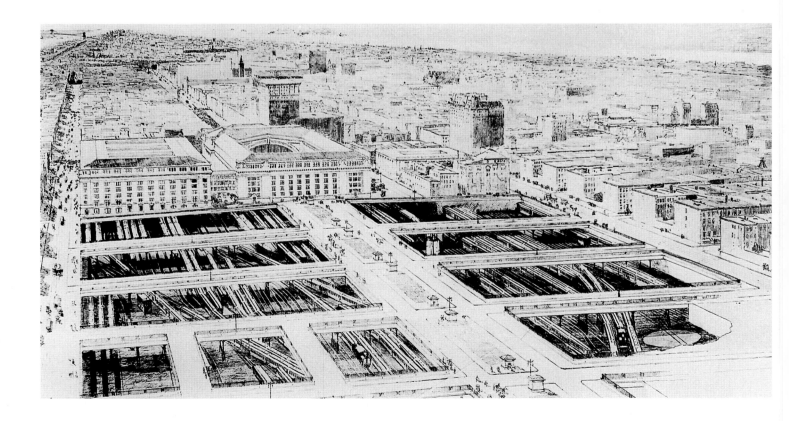

ABOVE: An illustration of the vast structure, open trackwork, and environs of New York's Grand Central Station—
before the underground tracks were covered over to improve the aesthetics and traffic of the surrounding area.

ABOVE: Although the overall concept is grand, sometimes it can be a problem to incorporate smaller items into a functional design—such as these ticket booths shown here at Grand Central II, New York, which must be easily found, but still comfortably human in scale.

ABOVE: A cross-cut rendering of New York's second Grand Central Station shows that this vast station extends many levels underground. The complex is an organizational masterpiece designed to maximize train and passenger capacity, as well as user convenience.

FOLLOWING PAGE: New York's Grand Central Station has public spaces to match its passenger capacity— it was designed to handle sixty-seven tracks serving more than six hundred trains a day on long distance and suburban routes.

passengers a day (a capacity still short of some London or Paris stations, which could handle a thousand trains and 200,000 passengers). But in New York this was achieved with minimum walking distances by arranging the tracks on two levels—long-distance express above and commuting-suburban below, linked by ramps.

All the facilities were related to the concourse. The platforms were now conceived of as just one more ancillary space from which passengers boarded trains, spending the minimum transit time between the train and the concourse, here 125 feet (38 meters) wide by 375 feet (114 meters) long by 120 feet (37 meters) high. Passengers were only called from the concourse to the platform as the train approached. This was a complex ensemble, offering a brilliant solution to the multiple circulation and spatial requirements. Although it became rather overshadowed by surrounding buildings externally, the station none the less retained an expressive and commanding unity of style.

Over time, sheds over the platforms in some of the large stations were replaced with "bush" type sheds: small, low sheds spanning only across two platforms and the tracks between, with large vents at the top to let out smoke. Still later these sheds were replaced with

open "butterfly-type" shelters, which merely protected the platforms from rain.

By the early twentieth century, the newer stations had become almost separate from the trains. As the concourse was now the station's main space, it became the focal point of the design. The first Pennsylvania Station, New York (McKim, Mead, and White, 1906–1910), had a plaza-like space, 150 feet (46 meters) high, open to the tracks below and linked at the same level to a grand, formal waiting room and a dramatic concourse with a glazed barrel vault worthy of a cathedral. At Washington, D.C.'s Union Railroad Station (D. H. Burnham, 1903–1907), the expectation of large numbers of visitors for national events led to a fine, vaulted concourse 760 feet (232 meters) long by 130 feet (40 meters)

RIGHT: A contemporary of Grand Central Station II, New York's first Pennsylvania Station was no less grand. Shown here is the waiting hall, which, as with Chicago's Union Station, paid homage to the architecture of the great Roman baths.

LEFT: Today's Grand Central Station in New York (the second on the site) was designed and built before the skyscraper era. It is more difficult today to see the heroic scale of the external form and decoration against the later tall buildings.

ABOVE: Union Station, Washington, D.C., is part of the vast civic complex of that city, and is linked by a grand boulevard to the Capitol. The architectural style and white granite are appropriately monumental.

LEFT: Architects frequently based their designs for the grand concourses and halls of railways stations on Gothic or classical sources. At Union Station, Chicago, the waiting hall is a replica of the ancient Roman baths of Caracalla.

RIGHT: A "palace of the people," the gilded halls and concourses at Union Station, Washington, D.C., are far removed from the grimy bustle of the earlier great train sheds.

wide across the ends of platforms. Here the concourse roof was externally expressed as the dominant space in the station. Entry is through a three-bay central portico in white Vermont granite, with triumphal arch overtones; a boulevard links the station directly to the Capitol. Chicago Union, the only one of Chicago's six major stations to have survived, has a waiting room modeled on the ancient Baths of Caracalla in Rome.

However impressive these monumental spaces were, by the 1920s there was little to distinguish a station from any other public building. External clock towers, which had a dual purpose—for the town and railway—were becoming lost as skyscrapers mushroomed in the downtown areas. The Union railway terminal at Cleveland (Graham, Anderson, Probst, and White, 1923—1930) followed the Broad Street example, building over the station a 700-foot (213-meter) tower, once the tallest building west of New York City.

But the most perfect plan from an architectural viewpoint must surely be that of Cincinnati (Fellheimer and Wagner, 1929–1933). Here a concourse 450 feet (137 meters) long acts as a bridge over the eight tracks, and is accessed by a huge semicircular entrance hall—an admirable expression of passenger movement. The semicircular arch of the entrance elevation itself echoes the plan form, albeit somewhat ponderously; the entrance hall is also semicircular in section. A raised external plaza provides the drop-off point that is now needed for cars, buses, and taxis, as the station replaced one on an earlier downtown site.

RIGHT: Union Station Cincinnati's concourse bursts into color internally—a surprise after the austere approach. In the center is the passageway to the concourse and platforms.

ABOVE: This historical photograph of Union Station, Cincinnati, shows the logical outcome of a hundred years of development—an efficient network of transportation hubs for carrying passengers and freight across a vast continent.

ABOVE: This elevation of Cincinnati's Union Station echoes the "gateway" theme ultimately derived from Euston's grand arch. This semicircular arch motif is echoed in the curving wing blocks and the water garden.

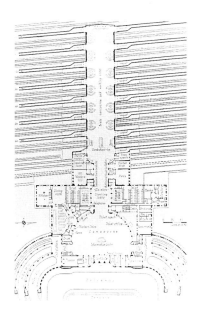

LEFT: The layout of Cincinnati's Union Station is the logical response to a station's function. Arrivals and departures are collected in the semicircular concourse, which gently funnels the traveler past the various facilities and into the waiting area, a bridge spanning the tracks and platforms below.

Modern Times

The sketches of "ideal" stations by St. Elia, 1913 (futurist) and Mendelssohn, 1914 (expressionist) epitomize the optimism of architects released from what they saw as the stylistic shackles of the previous century. Eliel Saarinen's Helsinki Station (1910–1914) is beautifully detailed, a clear modern statement of the functional form, with the barrel-vaulted roof of the concourse predominating externally. The stations at Karlsruhe (A. Sturzmacher) begun in 1908, and at Stuttgart (P. Bonetz and F. E. Scholer) in 1911 show contrasting approaches; the first has a beautiful, calm barrel-vaulted concourse utterly without pretension; the latter, powerfully expressionistic external masonry cladding, and the unusual arrangement of offices and waiting rooms on a central platform running parallel to the tracks. The Art-Nouveau facades of the Kursk Station in Moscow show the rapid spread of ideas, but the Beaux-Arts tradition also continued, as at Tokyo (1908–1914).

Electrification opened up new possibilities. Without soot, smoke, and steam a clean station could become a reality. And without the same need for ventilation, stations could even be sited in tunnels. The earlier limitations on underground rail-

ABOVE: Helsinki Station in Finland, designed by Eliel Saarinen (1910–1914), is a thoroughly consistent civic design executed in the grand manner. Here the station buildings form a U-shape around the tracks; the ornamental figures on the facade are by Emil Wilström.

LEFT: Whether for long distance or local travelers, modern railway architecture must accommodate itself to today's transportation needs. Shown here is the entrance to the subway station in Bielefeld, Germany.

RIGHT: The Moscow subway boasts stations that are vast in scale and lavish in style. Why not enjoy the journey to and from work? This is an opportunity sadly missed in most great cities.

ABOVE: Where nineteenth-century ornamental masterpieces no longer stand, modern railway structures display a typical twentieth-century utilitarian attitude. Shown here is the entrance to the station at Kassel-Wilhelmshöhe in Germany.

ways disappeared. The Underground in London and the Paris Métro became immensely important, doubling transportation capacity within the cities themselves. The Moscow subway, in a palatial baroque style, is unquestionably the grandest.

Reinforced concrete became the hallmark of the "modern" architectural style of the 1930s, ideally utilized in a pristine white, to match its cubist-inspired forms. Cast on-site in timber shuttering, it dispensed with the need for the complex patterns of lattices, rivets, and bolts that had been so characteristic of steel and iron architecture. Simple, pure, undecorated

form was its trademark. One of the earliest stations to take advantage of this material and its new aesthetics was Rheims La Marée in France (M. M. Limousins, 1930–1934). The concrete vaulted roof has ribs with perforated slots to allow the glazing to be cleaned. Concrete has become integral to twentieth-century architecture and style, used nowhere to better effect than at Naples (P. L. Nervi, 1950s).

Few large stations have been built since 1920—with the rail network fully in place only redevelopments and renovation have been required. Cross-circulation is the dominant consideration, and is typically expressed in concourses at a raised level. Rouen, France (A. Derraux, 1913–1928) is in Art-Nouveau style and, using ferro-concrete, is in some ways the archetypical "modern" station. The positioning of the tracks in a cutting between tunnels allowed the maximum use of bridges and levels to simplify circulation. The French Versailles Chantier shows an advanced functionalism similar

LEFT: There are several examples in Europe of new stations built to serve airports which provide a quick and efficient interchange between modes of transportation. Shown here is the Airport Station at Lyon.

LEFT: Today's urban architecture must address contrasting styles and eras. This photograph of a modern project proposal shows contemporary buildings sandwiching Victorian stations in London. On the left is St. Pancras; on the right is King's Cross—restrained and severe. Between is the proposal for the terminus for the high speed link with France via the Channel Tunnel.

to that of Cincinnati, but on a smaller scale. The opposite tendency is evident at the rebuilt Brunswick Station in Germany, which retains its single-sided approach and uses tunnels beneath the tracks to gain access to the further platforms, a common practice in Europe.

Although both were started in the 1930s, twenty years separate the completion of the stations at Milan (1930) and Rome (1950), and their ethos is ages apart. Milan is pure Beaux-Arts classicism, huge and monumental, "the masterpiece of the Fascist style." The main shed (of five) has a span of 236 feet (72 meters). In architecture and layout it harks back to the

past; it is designed to impress, not to make traveling easy. In 1957, the construction of the Rome station, interrupted by the Second World War, was restarted by Montuori and Calamini. They made a break with the past, despite including a section of old Roman wall in their building. At the head of the tracks is a fine concourse with a wave-like roof extending outwards as an entrance canopy. Behind this and obscured by it is a slim block of offices. The concourse is airy and light, and the restaurant off it opens onto its own garden. The monumental concourse of 30th Street Station, Philadelphia, is here given an informal, human scale.

LEFT: Architects von Gerkan, Marg & Partners have created an aesthetically pleasing and superbly functional multi-level space in the subway station at Bielefeld.

ABOVE: Changing transportation needs continually require new facilities, and not all match the heritage of the nineteenth century. The Darling Harbor Monorail in Sydney, Australia, is merged with a convention center.

FOLLOWING PAGE: The interior walkway at Lyon Airport Station gives passengers a view of the ultra-modern, wing-like, cement-ribbed roof designed by architect Santiago Calatrava.

Toward the Millenium

Despite the ubiquity of the rail networks and the continuing growth of cities, the twentieth century has seen a gradual but profound decline in their importance. Other forms of transportation—first cars and trucks, and then airplanes—have downgraded the status of the railways. In a car-owning era, rail transportation appeals only to those who want to travel between city centers. Air travel has further eroded the railway markets, especially for longer journeys—cross-continental railway journeys are for tourists only!

By the 1960s, much of the railway infrastructure was around one hundred years old. The costs of maintenance and

repair soared while revenues declined. The result has been rationalization—the selective retention and renovation of the viable parts of the rail network at the expense of the remainder.

Yet near paralysis of the road system by congestion is universal in large cities and is creating air pollution and environmental hazards. More powerful train engines have dramatically increased train speeds and reduced journey times. On many journeys trains can now beat the airlines by providing city-center departure and arrival without the tiresome need for airport transfers.

ABOVE: Lelystad Station, Netherlands. The local bus station is conveniently situated outside this small modern train station, allowing for easy transportation connections to areas not served by the railway.

RIGHT: Water dances in the fountain in front of Almere Central Station, one of the modern railway stations in the Netherlands.

Railway stations have followed these uncertain fortunes. Some have, sadly, been demolished, others have become ruins. Some have been redeveloped, some lovingly refurbished and restored, such as Liverpool Street in London. Redevelopment has usually included office and shopping malls, to generate the funds for the work. Thus at Euston, London, in the early 1960s, the famous and symbolic arch was destroyed, to be replaced by a vast and impersonal concourse space with office accommodation. Charing Cross, also in London, neglected for many years, was extensively redeveloped (Farrell, architect) in the late 1970s; however, it has acquired a new and distinctive identity as seen from the Thames, while retaining its facade to the Strand.

Where railways are accepted as essential to the commercial life of a city, they are regarded as a means of urban regeneration. At Bologna, Bofill's 1995 proposals include a new stepped piazza rising to the station and linking the medieval parts of the city on one side of the tracks to the nineteenth-century areas on the other—at least in intention.

A further set of station developments is designed to adapt and integrate the railway network more effectively with other transportation systems. At Vancouver, the station complex is combined with port facilities; in Zurich the railway line was rebuilt to stop at the new airport. Looking at the hall/concourse of the Gare d'Evry Couronnes, France (Hamburger, architect) it is hard to know whether it is part of a railway sta-

BELOW: An exterior view of Sloterdijk Station in Amsterdam. Unlike the stations of the past, where structural elements were covered with massive stonework and embellished with classical or Gothic ornaments, contemporary structures stress function over form.

ABOVE: The new terminal at Waterloo, designed by Nicholas Grimshaw, evokes the past era of the great rail sheds. Will this, as the London terminal of the new Channel Tunnel rail link with Continental Europe, herald a renaissance of railways in the twenty-first century?

LEFT: Albeit in a somewhat post-modern interpretation of a grand tradition, the shed at Sloterdijk Station in Amsterdam pays homage to the era of the great train sheds, such as that at York.

tion or an airport; and the Naples concourse is a forerunner of Foster's Stansted airport, although the materials and style are very different. Airport terminals have become the 1990s equivalents of the 1930s station concourses, from which their design is indirectly derived.

The advent of the high-speed train in Europe and elsewhere has produced some station development, notably at Lille, intended as a focal exchange point of this system. The new Waterloo terminal of the Channel Tunnel link in London is a sophisticated reinterpretation of the pioneer engineering of the great rail sheds. Although the span is insignificant at about 160 feet (50 meters), the new high-tech, lightweight structure and glazing (by Grimshaw) with its curved plan and perspectives looks forward as well as

back. Shinjuku Station in Tokyo is another mixed urban development as well as a high-speed bullet-train terminal.

It is paradoxical that later railway station designers only solved the problems they faced by sacrificing some of the vitality of the station as a unique form and experience. If, in this age of air travel, the railway experience is no longer so exciting, this can only be our loss. Will airports ever match the individuality and style of the great stations?

BELOW: Airports such as Stansted in the United Kingdom have replaced railway stations as the focal points of the world's transportation system. Their terminal buildings, with offices, services, and ancillary spaces organized around a large open concourse, are a direct development of the later railway stations.

INDEX